GROSS GRUB

Wretched Recipes That Look Yucky but Taste Yummy

By Cheryl Porter

Illustrated by Will Suckow

KidBacks™

RANDOM HOUSE 🏠 NEW YORK

Library of Congress Cataloging-in-Publication Data

Porter, Cheryl.
    Gross grub: wretched recipes that look yucky but taste yummy / by Cheryl
Porter; illustrated by Will Suckow.
        p. cm. — (Kidbacks)
      ISBN 0-679-86693-0
      1. Cookery—Juvenile literature. [1. Cookery.] I. Suckow, Will, ill. II. Title.
III. Series.
TX652.5.P667 1995
641.5—dc20   94-3455

Manufactured in the United States of America

10 9 8 7 6 5 4 3 2
KidBacks is a trademark of Random House, Inc.

Contents

Introduction

Does the thought of tuna casserole *make you want to commit a felony?* Do you *laugh* at the groceries your parents bring home? Have you been hagged at one or more times in the recent past for making *inappropriate dinner-table conversation?*

If you answered yes to any of the above, then you may be suffering from Bored (taste) Buds. *Do not despair.* There is help for people like you.

1. Strap on an apron.

2. Prepare any of the scientifically engineered bud-stimulating recipes in this cookbook.

3. Invite a few similarly taste-deficient family members or friends to dine with you.

4. Batten down the barf bags, *and stand back*—'cause from Brain Cell Salad to Blackberry Blackheads, the deliciously disgusting dishes in *Gross Grub* will make even the most blasé buds *bug* out!

SOME SAFETY TIPS

1. Ask an adult for permission before cooking any recipe.

2. Always wash your hands with soap and water *before* preparing food and *after* handling uncooked meat.

3. Tie back long hair and roll up loose sleeves to avoid having yourself catch on fire.

4. Wash all fruits and vegetables in cold water before preparing.

5. Make sure all pots, pans, and cooking utensils are clean before using.

6. Check all ingredients for freshness before using.

7. Ask an adult to help you use the stove, oven, electrical appliances, or any sharp kitchen tools, such as knives, peelers, graters, and scissors.

8. Place pots on burners before turning on the stove, and turn off the stove before removing pots from burners.

9. When cooking on the stove, keep pot handles turned away from you so the pots won't be knocked over accidentally.

10. Use thick, dry pot holders to handle hot pots, pans, plates, and cookie sheets. (Keep pot holders and dish towels away from heat and flames.)

11. Never handle an electrical appliance with wet hands or use one in a wet place.

12. When using an electric mixer, always turn off the motor and pull out the plug before lifting beaters out of the bowl.

13. Hold the lid down before turning on an electric blender. Never reach inside a blender with your hands; the blades are razor sharp!

14. Clean up countertops and utensils as you use them. To avoid breaking your neck, wipe up floor spills as soon as they happen.

15. Make sure your kitchen has a working fire extinguisher, and ask an adult to show you how to use it.

TERMS TO KNOW

blend - To combine ingredients completely together into one substance.

boil - To heat liquid until bubbles rise constantly to the surface and break.

chop - To cut food into small pieces.

colander - A large bowl with many small holes used to drain liquid from food, such as spaghetti.

core - To use a knife or carrot peeler in an up-and-down motion to remove the stem and core of a fruit or vegetable.

dice - To cut into pieces all the same size (usually about one-quarter inch).

flour - To cover a greased baking surface with a light layer of flour, shaking off the excess.

frying pan - A wide, shallow pan for frying.

grease - To spread a thin layer of butter, margarine, or oil over the inside surface of a pan, dish, or cookie sheet, to keep food from sticking.

mash - To break down food until it's creamy.

mix - To stir ingredients together evenly.

paring knife - A small, sharp knife with a smooth blade, used to remove skin from a fruit or vegetable.

peel or **pare** - To cut off the outer skin of a fruit or vegetable.

pinch - The amount of an ingredient you can pinch between two fingers.

preheat - To heat the oven to a desired temperature before putting food in to cook.

saucepan - A deep, narrow pan for heating and boiling.

separate - To pull apart or divide.

serrated knife - A sharp knife with a wavy blade edge, for slicing food with a tough surface.

simmer - To cook on low heat until a few bubbles rise gently to the surface and break.

slice - To cut food into layers or strips.

tongs - A pliers-like metal cooking utensil used for picking up hot foods.

whip - To beat rapidly in order to add air.

whisk - To rapidly move a wire whisk through food in a circular motion.

DE-GROSSING THE KITCHEN

1. Wash all pots, pans, and utensils in hot, soapy water. Wash knives separately, holding the handle of the knife, not the blade.

2. Check that the oven and stove burners are completely turned off when finished.

3. *Unplug* and wipe off all electrical appliances with a barely damp sponge or towel.

4. Carefully wipe down all countertops and the stove (avoiding any hot burners).

5. Sweep up crumbs and mop up any floor spills.

6. Carefully cover, label, and date all leftovers before storing in the refrigerator.

Measurements Every Gross Gourmet Should Know

3 teaspoons = 1 tablespoon

4 tablespoons = $\frac{1}{4}$ cup

8 tablespoons = $\frac{1}{2}$ cup

16 tablespoons = 1 cup

16 ounces = 1 pound

2 cups = 1 pint

4 cups = 1 quart

2 quarts = $\frac{1}{2}$ gallon

4 quarts = 1 gallon

8 tablespoons or $\frac{1}{2}$ cup butter = 1 stick butter

4 sticks or 2 cups butter = 1 pound butter

Unappetizers

Simple Pimples
(see page 22)

Slab o' Scabs
(see page 21)

Deviled Mice
(see page 16)

boogers-on-a-stick

Fingers tired and stomach growling? Don't despair.
Pick with a stick!

ingredients

- 1 (8-ounce) jar processed cheese spread (such as Cheez Whiz®)
- Green food coloring
- 25–30 pretzel sticks

tools you'll need

- Waxed paper
- Long-handled spoon
- Platter

1 With an adult's help, melt the processed cheese spread in the microwave oven or on top of the stove, according to directions on the jar.

2 Allow the cheese to cool slightly in the jar.

3 Using a long-handled spoon, carefully stir about three drops of green food coloring into the warm cheese, using just enough to turn the cheese a delicate snot green.

4 To form boogers: Dip and twist the tip of each pretzel stick into the cheese, lift out, wait twenty seconds, then dip again. When

cheese lumps reach an appealingly boogerish size, set pretzels booger-down onto a sheet of waxed paper. If the cheese in the jar begins to stiffen, simply reheat it.

5 Allow finished boogers-on-sticks to cool at room temperature for ten minutes, or until cheese is firm. Gently pull boogers off waxed paper and arrange on a serving platter.

Serves: 5 to 6 booger buddies

sicko serving suggestion
Place a bowl of chunky red salsa in the center of the platter so that guests can turn plain boogers into bloody ones!

crispy caterpillar cocoons

Does the thought of fresh squished insect larvae make your mouth water? Do you yearn to lap up a quivering pile of glistening yellow caterpillar goo? Why deny yourself? Tear into one of these crispy cocoons and let your taste buds take flight!

ingredients

- 1 (8-ounce) tube refrigerated crescent rolls
- 8 beef sausages (such as Brown & Serve®)
- 1 squeeze bottle yellow mustard

tools you'll need

- Frying pan
- Metal tongs
- Paper towels
- Knife
- Cutting board
- Carrot peeler
- Cookie sheet

1 With an adult's help, preheat the oven according to directions on the crescent-roll package.

2 Prepare the sausages according to the directions on the package. Use tongs to remove the cooked sausages from the frying pan and place them on paper towels. Allow to cool ten to fifteen minutes.

3 With an adult's help, carefully cut the sausages in half lengthwise. Then use the rounded tip of a carrot peeler to scoop out a long, shallow trough down the length of each half. Squeeze a thin line of mustard into each trough.

4 Separate the crescent-roll dough into its pre-cut triangle pieces, and lay them flat on an ungreased cookie sheet. To form insect larvae, take two sausage halves and, with their mustard-filled sides touching, put them together to form a whole. Place a whole larva at the wide end of each dough triangle, and roll up dough as you would regular crescent rolls. Pinch the ends and seams of the rolls closed.

5 Bake according to package instructions. (Allow the little buggers to cool fifteen to twenty minutes before chowing down on their tender torsos!)

Serves: 4 goo gobblers

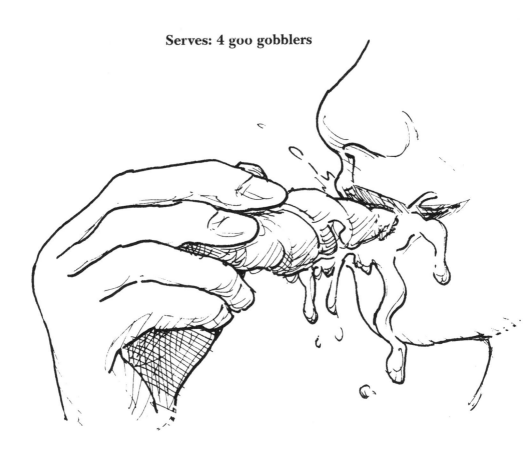

13

butchered snake bits with barbecue sauce

*Rustle up a rattler and taste life on the open range—
barbecue style!*

ingredients

- 1 (10-ounce) package rigatoni pasta
- 2 cans squirtable cheese spread
- 1 small jar barbecue sauce
- 16–20 whole black peppercorns
- 1 carrot

tools you'll need

- Large saucepan
- Colander
- Platter
- Carrot peeler
- Knife
- Toothpicks

1 With an adult's help, cook the pasta according to directions on package. Carefully drain the cooked pasta through a colander over the sink. Rinse the pasta in cold water and drain again.

2 To make snakes: Covering one end of a rigatoni with your finger (to prevent leakage), carefully fill each piece of pasta with cheese spread. Place six to eight cheese-filled rigatonis end to end on a serving platter, in a realistically curvy snake shape. (See illustration.) To form tails, simply pinch together the end of the last rigatoni on each snake with your fingers.

3 Using a toothpick, spread lines of barbecue sauce along the top of each snake for markings. To form heads, use barbecue sauce to glue two black peppercorn eyes onto the end opposite the tail of each snake.

4 Wash, dry, and carefully peel skin off carrot. When completely clean of skin, make one more peeling for each snake you have formed. At the narrow end of each peel, carefully cut out a long, thin triangle. (See illustration.) These are your snakes' forked tongues. Position tongues in mouths, and serve snakes with toothpicks so guests can stab at segments.

Serves: 10 to 12 flesh fanciers

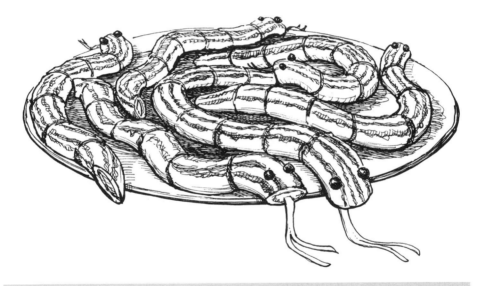

sicko serving suggestion

Assemble two or three snakes lying on their backs, as if they died in agony! Belly-up snakes should have no markings drawn on them, as snake bellies are generally a solid color. Allow one or two sidewinders to wriggle over the edge of your serving platter and onto a clean glass or Formica tabletop!

deviled mice

So why should Kitty have all the fun?

ingredients

- 8 eggs
- 4 ½ tablespoons mayonnaise
- 6 large lettuce leaves
- 16 pimiento-stuffed olives
- 1 tablespoon chocolate sprinkles

tools you'll need

- Large saucepan
- Knife
- Bowl
- Fork
- 64 toothpicks
- Platter

1 Gently place the eggs in a saucepan and fill it with water until the eggs are just covered. With an adult's help, bring the water to a boil over high heat. Turn the heat down to medium and allow to simmer for ten minutes.

2 Remove the pan from the heat and carefully drain off the hot water into the sink. Cover the eggs with cold water and set aside for five minutes.

3 Gently crack the eggs against a hard surface, then carefully peel off the shells. Slice each egg in half lengthwise. With clean fingers, scoop out the yolks and put them in a small bowl.

4 Mash the yolks with a fork until they are crumbly. Add mayonnaise and blend. Carefully fill the empty egg whites with yolk mixture.

5 Cover a platter with lettuce leaves, setting a leaf or two aside for garnish. Arrange the egg halves, *yolk side down,* on the leaves. These are your mice bodies. To give them each eyes and a nose, pull the pimiento out of an olive and cut it into three small pieces. Carefully insert two of the pieces at the top of the smaller end of the egg as eyes. Insert the third piece at the tip of the small end for a nose. Stick two toothpicks into each side of the nose for whiskers. Repeat for each mouse.

6 With an adult's help, cut thirty-two thin, lengthwise strips from several of the green olives. Stick two of these olive strips end to end onto the back end of each mouse to form tails. Out of the remaining olives, cut thirty-two small triangular ear pieces. (You should be able to cut at least four ears from each olive.) Then, using a knife, make two small slits above and behind each of the mice's eyes. Carefully wedge an olive ear piece into each slit.

7 To garnish: Tear small pieces of lettuce and position in front of the mice's mouths, as if they have been noshing. As a final touch, heap a pile of mouse droppings (chocolate sprinkles) on the platter to re-create an authentically tidy mouse toilette!

Serves: 4 rodent relishers

tomato hornworm wipe-outs

Why, look what Mommy dearest brought in from the garden. A nice, big, juicy tomato with a hornworm slithering out of it! Leave it to Mom to always pick a winner!

ingredients

- 1 cucumber
- 1 extra-large ripe tomato
- 1 (4-ounce) package string cheese
- 1 (8-ounce) container whipped cream cheese
- 1–2 tablespoons salad dressing

tools you'll need

- Carrot peeler
- Paring knife
- Cutting board
- Bowl
- Spoon
- Butter knife
- Plate

1 With an adult's help, use a carrot peeler to remove the cucumber skin. Discard the skin, and continue peeling long, thin strips the entire length of the cucumber until you reach the cuke's seedy core. Set these strips aside. Dice the seedy core into tiny pieces about one-half inch big, squeeze out excess liquid, and place in a bowl.

2 You now need to remove the top of the tomato, much as you would the top of a pumpkin to make a jack-o'-lantern. Ask an adult to do the following: Take a paring knife and carefully

poke it into the tomato, about one inch from
the stem, pointing the knife at a 30-degree
angle aimed downward and
toward the tomato's cen-
ter. With a sawing, up-and-
down motion, cut all the
way around the tomato.
Gently remove and discard
the tomato's "lid."

3 Using a spoon, scoop out the tomato's center, leaving a large,
bowl-shaped space inside the tomato. Chop these tomato
insides into tiny pieces, drain off excess juice, and add them to
the bowl of chopped cucumber.

4 Pull apart the pieces of string cheese into strips that are about
the width of a pencil. Cut each strip into thirds and set aside.

5 To make hornworms, use a butter knife to spread a thin layer
of cream cheese onto one side of a cucumber strip. Then,
using the cream cheese side as "glue," wrap the cucumber
strip in a coiling fashion around a piece of string cheese, from
one end of the cheese to the other. Repeat until all pieces of
string cheese are used, and set aside.

6 Blend the remaining cream cheese with one to two tablespoons of your favorite salad dressing, and stir into the
chopped cucumber and tomato. Spoon this mixture into your
hollowed-out tomato, and refrigerate any extra that won't fit.

7 Place the tomato on the center of a plate. Ask an adult to use a paring knife to carefully carve three or four holes, the same diameter as the worms, in various places on the tomato. Carefully insert worms into the holes, and arrange others on the plate.

Serves: Approximately 4 to 6 not-so-early birds

sicko serving suggestion

Cover the plate with torn-up lettuce leaves, and arrange worms crawling through gnawed-out holes. (Use cream cheese to seal one worm inside a folded leaf, as if it has made a cocoon!)

slab o' scabs

Don't just pick your scabs—stick them on toast for added zest!

ingredients

- 12–16 raisins
- 2 slices of bread
- Butter or margarine
- Seedless berry jam

tools you'll need

- Toaster
- Plate
- Butter knife

1 Tear raisins into variously sized, scab-like pieces and set aside.

2 Toast bread until golden brown.

3 Carefully place hot toast on a plate.

4 Spread each slice of toast first with butter or margarine, and then with jam. Artfully arrange scabs on jam and eat.

Serves: 1 wound worshiper

sicko serving suggestion

Surreptitiously place a raisin scab on the gauze pad of a sterile—*non-medicated*—bandage, and apply it to the clean, dry appendage of your choice. Then tell your intended victim that you're so hungry you could eat a scab. Whip off your bandage and chow down in front of them!

simple pimples

Scrap the zit cream! Pimple popping is fun, easy, and tasty, too.

ingredients

- Cherry tomatoes (allow approximately 2–4 tomatoes per person)
- Flavored soft cream cheese spread

tools you'll need

- Paper towels
- Carrot peeler or sharp knife
- Butter knife
- Serving platter

1 Rinse tomatoes in cold water and dry gently with paper towels.

2 Ask an adult to use a carrot peeler or sharp knife to core tomatoes. Drain excess tomato juice.

3 Using a butter knife, fill holes in tomatoes with cream cheese. Wipe excess cream cheese from the outside of the tomatoes with a clean, damp paper towel.

4 Give each pimple a gentle squeeze, and arrange on a platter.

Serves: As many pus-loving pals as your heart desires

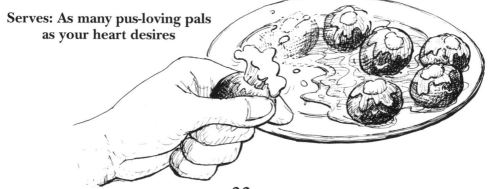

22

Septic Salads & Scummy Soups

Diaper Dump Porridge
(see page 32)

Dead Sea Soup
(see page 28)

Hairball Salad
with Saliva
Dressing
(see page 26)

brain cell salad

Can't think of what to serve your guests? A mound of quivering gray matter is always an intelligent choice!

ingredients

- 1 (6-ounce) package blueberry gelatin dessert mix (such as Jell-O Berry Blue®)
- 1 (16-ounce) container small-curd cottage cheese
- 1 (16½-ounce) can blueberries in syrup (or ¾ cup frozen blueberries, thawed)
- Blue food coloring

tools you'll need

- 2 mixing bowls
- Can opener
- Spoon
- 6 salad plates

1 With an adult's help, prepare gelatin according to the directions on the package. Chill for four to five hours, or until firm.

2 Scoop cottage cheese into a bowl. Drain and set aside the syrup from the blueberries. Add the berries to the cottage cheese and mix well. Add three drops food coloring to turn the cottage cheese a nice grayish color when blended.

3 To serve salad, place a few spoonfuls of firm gelatin (congealed brain fluids) onto individual plates. Top with a scoop of cottage cheese (brain tissue) mixture and serve.

Serves: 6 psycho surgeons

tortured tomatoes with bird-dropping dressing

It's thick. It's white. It's on the car windshield, and now it's on your salad! Go ahead. Do do the brave thing, and dig in!

ingredients

- 2 large *ripe* tomatoes
- 2 tablespoons crumbled blue cheese
- Roquefort dressing

tools you'll need

- Serrated knife
- Plastic food storage bag
- Plate
- 4 salad bowls
- Spoon

1 Wash the tomatoes in cold water, and with an adult's help, cut them into half-inch-thick slices.

2 Place the slices in a plastic bag. Squeeze out any extra air and close the bag tightly. Lay the bag on a clean plate placed in the sink. Now make a fist and gently pound the tomato slices until they look "tortured."

3 Divide the tortured tomatoes into four salad bowls, and sprinkle a half tablespoon of crumbled blue cheese into each bowl. Then, holding a spoon raised at least twelve inches from the salad bowls (to approximate the altitude of a low-flying bird), dribble a glob of Roquefort dressing onto each one.

Serves: 4 partying poopers

hairball salad with saliva dressing

Tired of the same old lettuce and tomatoes? Well, strap on a feed bag, kiddies, 'cause Kitty's thrown up some fabulously fiber-filled hairballs!

ingredients

- 1 large ripe avocado
- 2 cups alfalfa sprouts
- 5–6 large carrots, washed, peeled, and grated
- Italian dressing

tools you'll need

- Paring knife
- Spoon
- Mixing bowl
- Fork
- Carrot peeler
- Grater
- 4 salad bowls

1 With an adult's help, cut the avocado in half. Use a spoon to scoop out the single large pit.

2 Scoop the avocado meat out of its skin and into a bowl. Add alfalfa sprouts to the avocado meat and mash with a fork. (It is okay to leave some small lumps.) Set the mixture aside.

3 Divide the grated carrots between four salad bowls.

4 Using your clean fingers and a spoon, make walnut-size hairballs from the avocado mixture and arrange them on top of the grated carrots. Pour Italian "saliva" dressing over hairballs and serve.

Serves: 4 cat fanciers

sicko serving suggestion

Squeeze ribbons of chocolate icing "hairball medicine" out of a paper cone and onto the backs of your guests' hands, to be licked off for dessert.

dead sea soup

Straight from the unclean oceans of the world, this soup adds new meaning to the word "seasick"!

ingredients

- 1 celery heart and surrounding whitish leafy stalks
- 1 small jar artichoke hearts
- 1 (10 ½-ounce) can chicken and rice soup
- Blue and green food coloring
- 1 cup fish-shaped crackers

tools you'll need

- Knife
- Cutting board
- Large saucepan
- Spoon
- Soup ladle
- 4 soup bowls

1 With an adult's help, chop a celery heart into small pieces. Using clean hands, pull apart the surrounding whitish leafy stalks, leaving them long and stringy; these celery pieces will be your seaweed. Set the chopped and pulled-apart celery aside.

2 Drain the jar of artichoke hearts and, with an adult's help, cut the hearts into pieces about the size of a penny.

3 With an adult's help, prepare soup according to the directions on the can. Add the chopped artichoke, celery, and stringy stalks, and cook on medium high heat until soup comes to a boil. Turn heat to low and carefully add two to three drops

each of green and blue food coloring until the soup reaches an appropriately murky seawater color. Simmer for about five minutes, or until celery stems are limp.

4 Carefully ladle the hot soup into individual bowls, and sprinkle a quarter cup of fish crackers on top of each one. Encourage some of the floating celery seaweed to hang over the edge of bowls, and serve. (Artichoke pieces and rice from the soup will sink—just like real sediment of decayed plant and animal life!)

Serves: 4 fishy friends

29

homemade maggot stew

Show Mom how much you admire her cooking by whipping up
this hearty maggot stew—just like the kind she makes in those
little plastic containers pushed into the back of the fridge!

ingredients

- 2 tablespoons vegetable oil
- ¼ cup flour
- ½ teaspoon salt
- ½ teaspoon pepper
- ¼ teaspoon garlic powder
- 1 pound beef stew meat (pre-cut into one-inch chunks)
- 2 (14½-ounce) cans plain stewed tomatoes
- 1 (10½-ounce) can beef broth
- 1 teaspoon thyme
- 1 bay leaf
- 3–4 medium carrots
- 1 cup frozen or fresh green beans
- ¾ cup orzo pasta

tools you'll need

- Sharp knife
- Large stew pot with lid
- Plastic food storage bag
- Long-handled cooking spoon
- Carrot peeler
- Large saucepan
- Colander
- Slotted spoon
- 8 soup bowls
- Soup ladle

1 Place the oil in a large stew pot, and with an adult's help, turn
the heat on to medium low. Measure flour, salt, pepper, and
garlic powder into a plastic food storage bag, hold the top
shut, and shake the bag. Drop the meat cubes into the bag,
hold the top shut, and shake again. When the meat pieces are
well coated, pour the entire contents of the bag into the stew
pot. Turn the heat up to medium.

2 With an adult's help, use a long-handled spoon to turn the meat every three to five minutes, letting the pieces brown well on all sides. Cook until the meat begins to look crusty. Add the tomatoes, broth, thyme, and bay leaf to the pot. Bring the mixture to a boil, then turn the heat to low. Cover the pot with a lid, and let the stew simmer for an hour.

3 With an adult's help, peel the carrots and then cut them into small coins with a knife. When the stew has simmered for one hour, add the carrots and green beans to the pot. Cover and simmer for another forty-five minutes.

4 With an adult's help, cook the orzo in a saucepan according to the directions on the package. When the pasta is just tender, carefully drain it through a colander in the sink, shaking out any excess water. These are your maggots. Add them to the stew pot, then turn off heat and carefully remove the bay leaf with a slotted spoon. Serve the maggot stew in individual bowls.

Serves: 8 maggot munchers

sicko serving suggestion

Turn any meaty meal into a freaky feast by spreading a layer of orzo maggots *on top of* your roasted, baked, or boiled beast!

diaper dump porridge

Wait! Don't dump that diaper! Grab a bowl and whip up this perfect porridge. Go on, try it. There's no poo-pooing this meal.

ingredients

- 1 (10-ounce) can beef broth
- 1 tube of 8 refrigerated biscuits
- 1 (10-ounce) can chicken broth

tools you'll need

- 2 small saucepans
- Knife
- Slotted spoon
- Soup ladle
- 4 soup bowls

1 Pour the beef broth into a saucepan. Set aside, and don't add any water.

2 Remove the biscuits from the tube, separate them, and carefully cut each one in half. Then, using clean hands, sculpt the biscuit pieces into "dump" shapes.

3 Add the dumps to the beef broth. With an adult's help, place the dumps and broth over medium heat and cook until the mixture comes to a boil. Turn the heat to low, cover the pan with a lid, and simmer for fifteen to twenty minutes. Carefully check the broth level often. If there isn't enough liquid to keep the dumps afloat, carefully add water as needed.

4 Pour the chicken broth (diaper fluid) and one can of water into a second saucepan. With a slotted spoon, carefully transfer the cooked dumps from the beef broth and place in the chicken broth pan. Heat chicken broth according to directions on the can, stirring gently to preserve your dump shapes. Ladle into individual bowls and serve.

Serves: 4 diaper doodlers

sicko serving suggestion

When you're done eating, place a container of baby wipes on the table for guests to clean up with!

veggie vomit

Haul some hurl to your next potluck affair!

ingredients

- 1 (6-ounce) box lime gelatin dessert mix (such as Jell-O®)
- ¼ head cabbage
- 3 carrots, washed and peeled
- 1 (8-ounce) can crushed pineapple, drained
- 1 (11-ounce) can mandarin orange segments, drained

tools you'll need

- Grater
- Knife
- Mixing bowl
- Fork
- Plastic wrap

1 With an adult's help, prepare the gelatin according to directions on package. Refrigerate gelatin for two and one-half hours, or until partially set.

2 With an adult's help, grate approximately half a cup of cabbage and half a cup of carrots into a bowl. Add the drained pineapple and orange segments to the vegetables, and mash together with a fork until mixture looks well chewed.

3 Remove the partially set gelatin from the refrigerator. Dump the chewed vegetable mixture into the gelatin and stir gently with a fork. Cover the bowl with plastic wrap and put back in the refrigerator. Chill another two to four hours, or until mixture has the consistency of a grassy pile of gelatinous puke.

Serves: 8 to 10 chunk chompers

34

Main Curses

Pumpernickel
Pus Lumps
(see page 54)

Nose-Blow Burritos
(see page 40)

Penicillin Pizza
(see page 44)

queasy quail eggs

Rotten, smelly, and green with decay—they're delicious in a special way!

ingredients

- 1 dozen small boiling potatoes
- 1 1/2 cups frozen broccoli
- Salt
- 1 (8-ounce) jar processed cheese spread (such as Cheez Whiz®)

tools you'll need

- 1 large saucepan
- 2 small saucepans
- Fork
- Spoon
- Blender
- Mixing bowl
- Platter

1 Wash potatoes thoroughly in cold water, and place them in a large saucepan. Place frozen broccoli in a small saucepan. Cover both potatoes and broccoli with water, and add a pinch of salt to each pan.

2 With an adult's help, cook potatoes over high heat for approximately fifteen minutes, or until tender. Cook the broccoli about five minutes, or until tender. Carefully drain the cooked vegetables through a colander over the sink.

3 Put the broccoli in an electric blender and, with an adult's help, blend on medium speed for a few seconds, or until the broccoli is the consistency of thick salsa.

4 Place the cheese spread in a small saucepan and, with an adult's help, cook on low heat, stirring the cheese continuously until it's completely melted. The cheese can also be heated in a microwave oven, following the instructions on the jar.

5 Remove the cheese from the stove and pour it into a mixing bowl. Add the broccoli to the cheese, and mix with a spoon until the cheese is completely green.

6 Using a fork, spear the potatoes one at a time and dip them into the cheese mixture, covering each potato completely. Set the potatoes on a platter, spoon extra cheese mixture over them, and serve.

Serves: 4 to 6 foul fellows

sicko serving suggestion

Rotten eggs are the perfect side dish to serve with chicken or other poultry. Just ask Mom or Dad to rustle up a dead bird and bake it!

worm burgers

They wiggle with flavor!

ingredients

- 1¹/₂ cups mung bean sprouts
  (the thick, white kind)
- 1 pound ground beef
- 1 egg
- Salt and pepper to taste
- Mayonnaise
- Ketchup
- 6 hamburger buns

tools you'll need

- Mixing bowl
- Large frying pan
- Spatula
- Aluminum foil
- Platter

1 Wash sprouts (worms) in cold water. Using clean hands, mix one cup of the sprouts, the ground beef, and the raw egg together in a bowl. Reserve the remaining half cup of sprouts until later.

2 To form burgers: Pat a fist-sized lump of meat mixture between your palms until it's round, then press it between your hands to form a flat patty. You should have enough meat mixture to form five or six patties.

3 Place patties in a frying pan. Sprinkle them with salt and pepper, and with an adult's help, cook on medium heat until they are well browned underneath. Carefully turn the patties, season them again with salt and pepper, and cook until the second side is well browned. (Cover cooked burgers with aluminum foil to keep warm until all the patties are fried.)

4 Put cooked patties on open buns and serve with the extra half cup of worms sprinkled on top as a garnish. Don't forget the pus (mayonnaise) and blood (ketchup)!

Serves: 5 to 6 worm slurpers

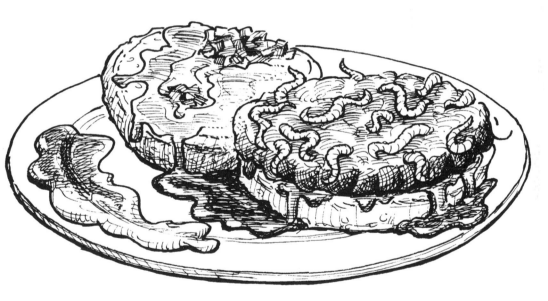

sicko serving suggestion

Use a clean hole puncher to punch wormholes in lettuce garnish!

nose-blow burritos

The perfect dish to feed your snottiest friends!

ingredients

- 2 medium tomatoes
- 1 pound ground beef
- 1 ($^1/_2$-ounce) package burrito or taco seasoning
- 1 (30-ounce) can refried beans
- 8–10 burrito-size soft flour tortillas
- 2 (8-ounce) containers guacamole dip
- 1 (16-ounce) container sour cream

tools you'll need

- Knife
- Cutting board
- 3 bowls
- Frying pan
- 5 spoons
- Spatula
- Small saucepan

1 With an adult's help, dice the tomatoes into small pieces, and place in a bowl.

2 With an adult's help, place the ground beef in a frying pan, sprinkle with the burrito or taco seasoning, and sauté on medium heat until it's well browned. Cover and set aside.

3 With an adult's help, cook the beans in a saucepan on low heat, stirring occasionally. When the beans are hot, gently combine them with the cooked ground meat in a clean bowl.

4 To build burrito beaks: Set one tortilla on a dinner plate. Spoon an approximately one-and-one-half-inch-wide strip of guacamole dip (rancid mucus) down the center of the tortilla. On top of that, spoon a strip of sour cream (fresh mucus), a strip of chopped tomatoes (bloody nose chunks), and finally, a strip of beans and beef boogie mixture.

5 Tightly fold the left and right sides of the tortilla over your ingredients, then tuck the lower third of the whole burrito under itself, making a triangular nose shape. (See illustration.) With an adult's help, use a sharp knife to cut out two large holes for nostrils. Gently squeeze the nose from the top to make the nose wider at the base. As you squeeze, snot should drip out of the nostrils and onto your plate!

Serves: 8 to 10 little buggers

sicko serving suggestion
Instead of napkins, set each guest's place with an individual-size packet of facial tissues!

puked-up potatoes

Why flush all that good vomit down the toilet when it makes the perfect side dish?

ingredients

- 1 medium carrot
- 4 medium potatoes
- 3 celery stalks
- $\frac{1}{2}$ cup frozen green beans
- Pinch of salt
- 1 (12-ounce) jar turkey or chicken gravy
- 3 tablespoons butter
- $\frac{1}{2}$ cup milk

tools you'll need

- Carrot peeler
- Knife
- Cutting board
- Small saucepan
- Large saucepan
- Potato masher
- 2 serving dishes

1 With an adult's help, carefully peel carrots and potatoes. Chop the carrots and celery into small pieces, and the potatoes into one-inch cubes.

2 Place the carrots, celery, and green beans in a small pan, and the potatoes in a larger one. Cover both with water and add a pinch of salt to each. With an adult's help, set the two pans over medium heat until they come to a boil. Turn heat to medium low and simmer carrots, celery, and green beans for about five to seven minutes, and the potatoes for about ten minutes, or until the contents are soft but not mushy. Carefully drain the water out of each pan, and set the potatoes aside.

42

3 Pour the gravy into the pan of carrots, celery, and beans. Return the pan to the stove, and with an adult's help, cook on low heat, stirring often, until hot.

4 While the gravy heats, add the butter and milk to the pan of potatoes. Mash potatoes in the pan until they are fairly lump-free.

5 Place a lump of mashed potatoes on a plate, then cover with a ladle of pukey gravy.

Serves: 6 hurlers

sicko serving suggestion

Almost any meal tastes better when you heave puke on it! To create a realistically splattered tableau, place a plate full of food in sink. Then take a large spoonful of gravy and, with a flick of the wrist, fling it onto the food. Repeat until the desired effect is achieved.

penicillin pizza

Why take a pill when you can make a pie?

ingredients

- 6 English muffins
- 1 (14-ounce) jar pizza sauce
- 2 cups shredded mozzarella cheese
- 3 tablespoons grated Parmesan cheese
- Yellow, green, and red food coloring

tools you'll need

- Cookie sheet
- Spoon
- Bowl
- Plastic sandwich bag

1 Separate the muffins into halves, and arrange them ragged sides up on an ungreased cookie sheet. (Use two cookie sheets, if necessary, to keep muffins from touching each other.)

2 Spoon a thin layer of pizza sauce on top of each muffin, then cover the sauce with a layer of shredded mozzarella cheese. Set the pizzas aside.

3 Pour the Parmesan cheese into a small bowl, then sprinkle with five drops each of yellow, green, and red food coloring. Use clean fingers to mix the cheese and food coloring until

it's an even shade of mold green. (To avoid staining your fingers green, slip a small, clean plastic sandwich bag over them.) Set mold aside.

4 With an adult's help, broil the pizzas for two to three minutes. When the cheese has melted and is starting to brown, take the pizzas out of the oven and let them cool for about one minute.

5 Carefully sprinkle mold on top of the hot pizzas. Allow pies to cool slightly before you slip on a lab coat and serve.

Serves: 6 peaked patients

cat litter casserole

It's purrr-fect for any occasion!

to make cat dumps

- 1 cup baking mix (such as Bisquick®)
- 1 cup shredded Cheddar cheese
- 1 pound ground beef, turkey, or pork sausage

to make litter

- 2 cups long-grain rice
- 3 ¾ cups water
- 2 teaspoons salt
- 2 tablespoons butter or margarine

tools you'll need

- Large mixing bowl
- Rectangular baking pan
- Deep saucepan with lid
- Fork
- Paper towels
- Large spoon

1 To make dumps: With an adult's help, preheat the oven to 350 degrees. Using clean hands, mix together the dry baking mix, shredded cheese, and ground sausage in a large bowl. Mold pieces of this mixture into variously sized/shaped cat dumps. (See illustration.)

2 Place dumps so they don't touch each other in an ungreased rectangular baking pan. (Use two baking dishes if they don't all fit.) With an adult's help, bake dumps at 350 degrees for about twenty minutes, or until the dumps are brown, firm, and slightly crusty.

3 While the meat cooks, put all four litter ingredients into a large saucepan. Then, with an adult's help, heat on high until the water comes to a boil. Stir, turn heat to low, and cover the pan. Simmer without lifting the cover for fourteen minutes.

4 With an adult's help, remove the saucepan from the stove and carefully (to avoid having your face melted away by the steam), lift off the cover. Break apart, or "fluff," the rice with a fork, and set pan aside.

5 When the dumps are done, carefully transfer them from the baking dish onto paper towels to drain.

6 Spoon the rice and dumps into the now empty baking dish, leaving some dumps partially uncovered, the way Kitty does when he or she is in a hurry.

Serves: 8 to 10 litterbox lovers

sicko serving suggestion

Talk an adult into buying you a *brand spanking new* stainless steel cat box pooper scooper to use—*exclusively*—as a Cat Litter Casserole serving spoon!

spit-wad sandwiches

Finally. A use for spit wads even a Home Ec teacher would applaud!

ingredients

- 2 bread slices
- Creamy peanut butter
- 2 large marshmallows

tools you'll need

- Butter knife
- Plate

1 Spread each slice of bread with a thin layer of peanut butter.

2 Using clean fingers, pull apart marshmallows into many tiny spit-wad-sized pieces.

3 Press the marshmallow wads into the peanut-buttered bread slices.

4 Put the two slices together (with wad-enhanced sides facing each other), and enjoy.

Serves: 1 who wuvs spit wads

sicko serving suggestion

Make spit-wad place cards for your next sit-down affair! Write guests' names on torn pieces of notebook paper with a pencil. Place a small amount of vegetable oil in a bowl, and dip paper pieces into it until completely covered. Crumple papers into balls and place on small plates at each setting. Your guests will just *love* uncrumpling these slimy wads to find their seats.

chicken pox pancakes

What better way to celebrate an epidemic!

ingredients

- Strawberries
- 1 box pancake mix (and ingredients listed on package)
- Bananas
- Powdered sugar

tools you'll need

- Knife
- Cutting board
- Mixing bowl
- Large flat skillet
- Spatula
- Individual plates

1 With an adult's help, chop the berries into small chunks, allowing one to two strawberries per pancake face. Set aside.

2 With an adult's help, prepare pancakes according to the directions on the package. When the pancakes are done, place each serving in a stack on a separate plate.

3 For every two stacks of pancakes, you need to peel one banana. Carefully slice off the two ends of the banana, and put one on top of each stack for a nose. Then cut two thin slices from one end of the banana and two thin slices from the other end. Place these on the stacks for eyes. Slice what's remaining of the banana in half lengthwise, so you get two long, curved pieces. Use one piece per stack for a mouth.

4 Arrange the strawberry-chunk chicken pox all around each face. Use clean fingers to drop a pinch of powdered sugar on each strawberry pox for a tasty bit of pus.

Serves: As many little polka-dotted people as your heart desires

maggottini alfredo

A sensationally slimy supper. Bug appetito!

ingredients

- ½ package spaghettini
- 7 tablespoons butter
- 1 (15-ounce) can small white beans
- ½ teaspoon salt
- Pinch of pepper
- 4 tablespoons flour
- 2 cups half-and-half

tools you'll need

- Large pot
- Colander
- Cooking spoon
- 2 small saucepans
- Large serving dish
- 2 serving forks

1 With an adult's help, cook spaghettini in a large pot according to directions on package. Carefully drain spaghettini through a colander over the sink. Rinse the pasta in the colander with fresh hot water, drain thoroughly, then put the pasta back into the large pot, away from heat. Add three tablespoons of butter to the pasta, stir, and cover the pot.

2 Pour the beans (maggot eggs) and their liquid into a small saucepan, and with an adult's help, cook on medium heat. When the liquid comes to a boil, carefully drain the beans through a colander into the sink. Set aside.

3 Place the remaining four tablespoons of butter in a second saucepan, and with an adult's help, melt over low heat. Add salt and pepper to the melted butter, and gradually stir in the flour until smooth. Slowly stir in half-and-half, and continue heating sauce, stirring constantly, until it's thickened and slimelike.

4 Add the beans to the sauce, stirring until they are well coated. Arrange the warm pasta in a serving dish, then pour the slimed maggot eggs over the pasta. Use two forks to gently toss pasta and maggot sauce together, then serve.

Serves: 6 larvae lovers

sicko serving suggestion

Maggottini Alfredo makes the perfect romantic dinner! Pop Pavarotti into the CD player (*good luck!*), dim the lights, and toast your special someone with a sparkling glass of Ralph's Retch (page 58). Now, *that's amore!*

snouts 'n beans

Grab a few friends and pig *out on this tasty treat!*

ingredients

- 2 (16-ounce) cans plain baked beans
- 1 teaspoon Worcestershire sauce
- $1/4$ cup brown sugar
- 2 tablespoons barbecue sauce
- 1 tablespoon teriyaki sauce
- 8 beef knockwursts

tools you'll need

- 2 small saucepans
- Large spoon
- Cutting board
- Knife
- Carrot peeler
- Tongs or slotted spoon
- Paper towels
- Shallow serving dish

1 With an adult's help, empty the cans of baked beans into a saucepan. Add the Worcestershire sauce, brown sugar, barbecue sauce, and teriyaki sauce to the beans. Stir and set aside.

2 With an adult's help, slice off the ends of each knockwurst. (You do not need the ends for this recipe.) Then slice knockwursts into equal segments about one inch long, making each cut at the same slight angle. (See illustration.) With the round tip of a carrot peeler,

carefully hollow out two deep, round nostril holes on one side of each segment.

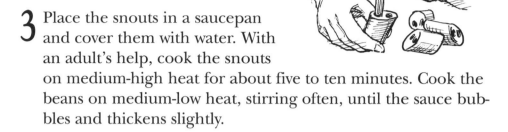

3 Place the snouts in a saucepan and cover them with water. With an adult's help, cook the snouts on medium-high heat for about five to ten minutes. Cook the beans on medium-low heat, stirring often, until the sauce bubbles and thickens slightly.

4 Using tongs or a slotted spoon, carefully remove the snouts from the hot water and place them on paper towels to drain. Pour the hot beans into a serving dish and arrange the drained snouts on top, nostrils up.

Serves: 4 to 6 little porkers

sicko serving suggestion
Dab pickle relish pig boogers in your knockwurst nostrils!

pumpernickel pus lumps

A pusitively gourmet alternative to the cheese sandwich!

ingredients

- 1 ($^3/_4$-ounce) jar capers
- 1 (4-ounce) tub whipped cream cheese
- 8 slices pumpernickel bread

tools you'll need

- Colander
- Bowl
- Spoon
- Toaster
- Butter knife

1 Carefully drain the capers through a colander over the sink. Place the drained capers in a bowl.

2 Scoop the cream cheese into the bowl of capers and mix gently.

3 With an adult's help, toast the bread. Spread each slice with a generous glop of pus lumps, and serve, open-faced, immediately.

Serves: 4 infectious friends

sicko serving suggestion

With the right attitude, you can turn even the most inoffensive fare into a foul feast. Next time Mom or Dad roasts a beast, dribble nontoxic fake blood from the corners of your mouth and offer to carry the quivering slab to the dining-room table!

Filthy Fluids

Day-Old Bathwater
(see page 56)

Sewer Soda
(see page 62)

Infectious Fluid Frappé
(see page 61)

day-old bathwater

Need to quench the thirst of a party crowd? Why not take that funky bathwater sitting in your tub since yesterday and serve it up in a punch bowl? People will soak it up!

ingredients

- 1 (12-ounce) can frozen lemonade
- 1 (12-ounce) can frozen pink lemonade
- 1 (12-ounce) can frozen limeade
- ½ gallon rainbow sherbet

tools you'll need

- Ice cream scooper or large spoon
- Mixing bowl
- Long stirring spoon
- Large punch bowl
- Ladle
- Cups

1 Approximately forty-five minutes before party time, set cans of lemonade and limeade and the container of rainbow sherbet out to thaw. After fifteen minutes, scoop out half of the sherbet container's contents and place it in a mixing bowl. Stir until it is blended into a brownish color. (Place the remaining sherbet back in freezer.)

2 Prepare the lemonades and limeade according to the directions on the cans, and pour into a punch bowl.

3 Carefully float spoonfuls of the brown blended sherbet on top of the lemonade mixture, spreading it around to look like dirty brown suds. Do not stir. Use a ladle to serve punch in cups.

Serves: About 30 dirty, non-bathing buddies

sicko serving suggestion
Float a handful of green, yellow, and white after-dinner mints (tiny bars of soap) on top of your scummy punch!

ralph's retch

Poor Ralph, he's retched again! Maybe it was those six snow cones and four cotton candies he ate before going on the Ferris wheel?

ingredients

- 1 (3-ounce) box strawberry gelatin dessert mix (such as Jell-O®)
- 40 ice cubes
- 2 (12-ounce) cans strawberry soda

tools you'll need

- Mixing bowl
- Shallow 9 x 12 baking pan
- Butter knife
- Blender
- Spoon
- Tall glasses
- Iced-tea spoons

1 With an adult's help, prepare the gelatin according to directions on package. Pour into a shallow baking pan and chill until firm (about three hours).

2 Remove the gelatin from the refrigerator. Using a dull knife, make as many cuts as possible across the length and width of the pan, forming tiny cubes.

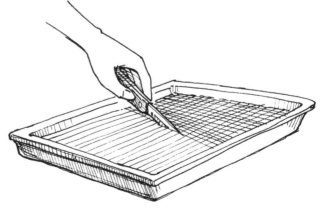

3 With an adult's help, grind ice cubes in a blender.

4 Spoon alternating thin layers of crushed ice and gelatin pieces into tall glasses, filling them about two inches away from tops. Slowly pour strawberry soda into each glass until full, then stir gently. Serve retch with iced-tea spoons, so your guests can get at every chilly glob.

Serves: 4 chunk munchers

sicko serving suggestion

Almost any cooked food can look like puke if you grind it for a few seconds in a blender. (And it makes for a tasty sandwich spread!)

fabric softener smoothie

The perfect blue goo for guzzling in front of Granny!

ingredients

- 7–8 ice cubes
- 1 cup milk
- 1 large scoop vanilla ice cream
- Blue food coloring

tools you'll need

- Blender
- Ice cream scooper
- Tall glass

1 With an adult's help, grind seven to eight ice cubes in a blender.

2 Add milk to the crushed ice, and blend on low speed for ten seconds. Add one large scoop of ice cream and blend again for about thirty seconds.

3 Slowly add about eight drops of food coloring to blender, mixing after every couple of drops, until smoothie is the color of your favorite fabric softener.

Serves: 1 downy dude

infectious fluid frappé

A cup of pus sounds good to us!

ingredients

- 8 maraschino cherries
- 1 quart eggnog
- 1 (3-ounce) box lime gelatin dessert mix (such as Jell-O®)
- Nutmeg

tools you'll need

- Knife
- Cutting board
- Blender
- 8 small dessert glasses

1 With an adult's help, chop the cherries into small bits.

2 Pour the eggnog and gelatin powder into a blender. With an adult's help, blend for one minute, or until the gelatin is completely dissolved and the eggnog is a uniform gangrenous green color.

3 Pour the green ooze into eight glasses. Drop cherry-chunk blood clots on top of each, and sprinkle with powdered plasma (or nutmeg).

Serves: 8 wittle wound wuvers

sewer soda

Don't let dirty dishwater, soapy bath suds, and toilet flushables go to waste! Recycle your savory sewage into a chunk-filled, tasty drink instead.

ingredients

- 1 quart chocolate–chocolate-chip ice cream
- $^3/_4$ cup (12 tablespoons) chocolate syrup
- 1 liter club soda

tools you'll need

- Large spoon
- 4 tall glasses
- Straws
- Iced-tea spoons

1 Let ice cream sit at room temperature until it is easy to scoop.

2 Spoon softened ice cream into tall glasses until about halfway full. Pour, or squeeze, about three tablespoons of chocolate syrup into each glass.

3 Slowly fill glasses almost to the top with club soda, and stir well with spoon. Serve with a straw *and* a tall spoon for excavating those luscious brown lumps!

Serves: 4 sewage slurpers

sicko serving suggestion

To make this slop especially disgusting, plop an unwrapped Tootsie Roll into each glass!

Squeamish Sweets

Dutch Dandruff
(see page 74)

Pathology Pound Cake
(see page 77)

Flat Cat Cookies
(see page 66)

liposuctioned lard

Wrap your lips around a lumpy load of sucked-out fat!

ingredients

- 2 large eggs
- 3 tablespoons sugar
- 1 1/2 cups milk
- 1/2 teaspoon vanilla extract
- Small pinch of salt
- 1 1/2 cups mini marshmallows

tools you'll need

- Medium-size mixing bowl
- Electric mixer
- Glass measuring cup
- 6 custard cups
- Large frying pan with lid
- Pot holder

1 With an adult's help, beat the eggs and sugar in a medium-size bowl until well blended. Add the milk, vanilla, and salt, and mix well. Use a glass measuring cup to divide the mixture evenly among six custard cups.

2 Place the custard cups in a large frying pan and fill the pan with water to about one-half inch from the top of the cups. With an adult's help, place the pan on medium heat, bringing the water to a simmer. Turn heat down to low

and cover the pan with a lid, and continue to let water simmer for ten minutes. Then turn off heat.

3 With an adult's help, carefully remove the cups from the water. Allow the custard to cool for five minutes, then gently stir one-quarter cup of marshmallow fat lumps into each cup, making sure all the lumps are coated with custard. Refrigerate cups for one to two hours, or until well chilled.

Serves: 6 lard lovers

flat cat cookies

Dad slams on the brakes, but it's too late. The Vista Cruiser has flattened the neighbor's kitty. Don't despair. Cats do have nine lives, and Dad's nailed tonight's dessert!

ingredients

- 1 (20-ounce) package refrigerated sugar cookie dough
- 1–2 tablespoons flour
- Red cinnamon candies
- Seedless strawberry jam

tools you'll need

- Rolling pin
- Butter knife
- Spatula
- Cookie sheet
- 2 spoons
- Wire cooling rack

1 With an adult's help, preheat oven to the temperature specified on the cookie dough package.

2 Sprinkle flour on a clean, flat surface, and roll out the cookie dough slightly thicker than what the directions on package call for. Then, using a butter knife, cut out cookies in the shape of flattened cats. (See illustration.) Use a large spatula to carefully transfer cats to a cookie sheet. Reroll spare dough pieces and cut out more cookies until all the dough has been used.

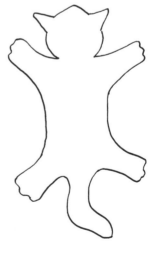

3 Bake cookies according to the directions on the package. While they're cooking, count out enough cinnamon candies to put two eyes and one nose on each cat cookie. Carefully flatten the candies between the back and front of two spoons and set aside.

4 Allow the cookies to cool on the cookie sheet about three minutes, and then press two candies in about the middle of each head, and one at the very tip of each nose. (See illustration.) Use the spatula to transfer cookies to a wire rack to continue cooling. Dribble jam here and there on each cookie for blood.

Makes approximately 3 dozen kitty road kill specimens

sicko serving suggestion

Instead of making each cookie in a perfect flat cat shape, cut out a few who are missing a limb and/or tail. Why not even sever a head or two? Drip jam blood at stumps for an authentically dismembered look.

toasted tongues

Sweet crunchy tongues you can stick out at anyone . . . even your teacher!

ingredients

- 6 egg whites
- 1 cup sugar
- Red food coloring
- Pink or red cake crystals

tools you'll need

- 2 small bowls
- Large mixing bowl
- Spoon
- Wire whisk or electric mixer
- Parchment paper (white, non-waxed paper for baking)
- Cookie sheet
- Popsicle sticks
- Spatula
- Toothpicks

1 With an adult's help, position an oven rack on the lowest shelf, and preheat the oven to 200 degrees.

2 Separate the whites from the yolks of the eggs into two small bowls. (Remove any yolk bits from the bowl of whites with a spoon.)

3 Using a wire whisk or, with an adult's help, an electric mixer, rapidly beat the egg whites until they form stiff peaks. Slowly sprinkle spoonfuls of the sugar onto the whites, and continue beating until the entire cup of sugar has been added. The whites should now form stiff, shiny peaks. Add two to three drops of red food coloring to the whites and whisk until the meringue is uniformly pink.

4 Place a sheet of parchment paper on a cookie sheet.

5 To form tongues: Spoon about three tablespoons of meringue in the shape of a tongue onto the parchment paper. (Tongues should be about as long as a Popsicle stick.) Press a Popsicle stick gently into the center of the tongue (as shown in diagram), leaving about two inches of clean stick hanging out the bottom. Spoon about three table-spoons more meringue on top of the stick, sculpting the tongue into a lifelike shape. Repeat until all the meringue is used. Using a toothpick, draw a line down the middle of each tongue, and then sprinkle them lightly with taste buds (pink cake crystals).

6 Bake on low rack in oven for about three hours, or until tongues are completely dry to the touch. Allow them to cool completely before carefully lifting them off the paper.

Makes about 12 little lickers

sicko serving suggestion

To serve *coated* tongues, use a tooth-pick to spread a thin layer of mucus (marshmallow topping) down the length of lickers.

blackberry blackheads

Few things are more satisfying in life than popping a great big zit. But why should adolescents have all the fun? The next best thing to zapping a zit is eating one!

ingredients

- 2 sticks ($1/2$ pound) plus 1 tablespoon butter, at room temperature
- $2/3$ cup sugar
- 2 egg whites
- 4 cups all-purpose flour
- Blackberry jam (with seeds)

tools you'll need

- Mixing bowl
- Large spoon (or electric mixer)
- Pastry brush
- Cookie sheet
- Spatula
- Wire cooling rack
- Small spoon

1 With an adult's help, preheat the oven to 325 degrees.

2 Beat two sticks of softened butter in a mixing bowl until creamy. Mix in the sugar a little at a time until all the sugar has been used.

3 Add the egg whites and flour to the butter and sugar. Beat until the dough is well blended.

4 Dip a pastry brush into the tablespoon of softened butter, and lightly brush a very thin layer onto a cookie sheet.

5 With clean hands, roll the dough into golf-ball-size balls. Flatten the balls slightly, and using your thumb, press a dime-size dent into the middle of each one. Place cookies, dent side up, on the buttered cookie sheet about one inch apart, and with an adult's help, bake for twelve minutes or until golden brown.

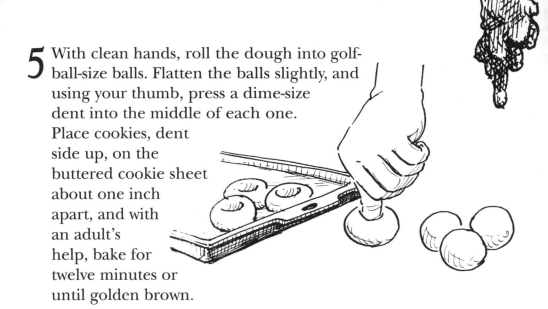

6 Allow the cookies to cool on the cookie sheet for a few minutes before moving them with the spatula to a wire rack. When the cookies are completely cooled, use a small spoon to fill the dent in each one with jam.

Makes about 3½ dozen blackheads

green grassy cow patties

Moo-ve over, Bessie! Now anyone can enjoy hot 'n' steamy cow pies in the convenience of their own home.

ingredients

- 1 (3-ounce) package lime-flavored gelatin dessert mix (such as Jell-O®)
- 1 cup hot water
- 1 cup sweetened shredded coconut
- 2 sticks ($^1/_2$ pound) butter, at room temperature
- $^2/_3$ cup firmly packed brown sugar
- $^1/_4$ cup granulated sugar
- 2 eggs
- 2 tablespoons milk
- 2 teaspoons vanilla extract
- $1\,^3/_4$ cups all-purpose flour
- 1 teaspoon baking soda
- $^1/_2$ teaspoon salt
- $2\,^1/_2$ cups old-fashioned rolled oats
- 1 cup chopped walnuts
- 1 cup currants

tools you'll need

- 2 small bowls
- Large mixing bowl
- Slotted spoon
- Paper towels
- Large spoon
- Cookie sheet
- Spatula
- Wire cooling rack

1 With an adult's help, preheat the oven to 375 degrees.

2 Mix the gelatin powder with the hot water in a small bowl. Stir until the gelatin is dissolved. Add the shredded coconut, stir again, and set the bowl aside.

3 Beat the butter and brown and white sugars in a large mixing bowl until creamy. Add the eggs, milk, and vanilla, and beat again. Set aside.

4 Combine the flour, baking soda, and salt in a small bowl. Add this to the wet ingredients in the large mixing bowl, and stir well. Add the oats, nuts, and currants to the dough and mix.

5 With a slotted spoon, separate the shredded coconut from the gelatin, and set the coconut on a few paper towels to drain. Place another two paper towels on top of the coconut and press, squeezing out any extra liquid. (The leftover gelatin is not needed for the rest of this recipe. You may add one cup of cold water to it and chill in the refrigator for a separate dessert.) Mix the now-green coconut into the dough.

6 Spoon out tablespoon-sized lumps of dough and place them on an ungreased cookie sheet one to two inches apart. With an adult's help, bake for nine to ten minutes, until golden brown. Allow lumps (which should now be shaped like steaming patties) to cool on cookie sheet for one minute. Then, using a spatula, lift the patties off the sheet and onto a wire rack to cool completely.

Makes about 5 dozen infested treats

73

dutch dandruff

A delicious dander-dusted cake that is head and shoulders above the rest!

ingredients

- Vegetable shortening
- Flour
- 1 (18½-ounce) box devil's food cake mix (plus those ingredients listed on package)
- 1 (16-ounce) can dark chocolate frosting
- Maraschino cherries
- 1 fruit roll (such as strawberry, raspberry, or cherry Fruit Roll-Ups®)
- 1 (3½-ounce) can sweetened coconut flakes

tools you'll need

- Mixing bowl
- Electric mixer
- 2 (9-inch) round cake pans
- Wire cooling rack
- Knife
- Heavy-duty plastic food storage bag
- Scissors
- Cake plate

1 With an adult's help, preheat the oven to the temperature shown on the cake mix package.

2 Grease the inside of both cake pans with vegetable shortening, then lightly coat greased surfaces with flour. Prepare, and with an adult's help, bake cake mix in the two pans according to package directions. After removing the cake from the pans, allow the layers to cool on a wire rack for at least one-half hour.

3 Place one of the layers upside down on a cake plate. Spread a thin layer of frosting on the top only, then carefully place the second cake layer right side up on top of the first layer.

4 Fill a heavy-duty plastic food storage bag with the rest of the frosting, and twist the top tightly shut. Using a scissors, cut off one tiny bottom corner of the bag.

5 To decorate: Think of the top of the cake as the top of a human head, and imagine a part running down its middle. Now, using the plastic bag of icing as a pastry bag, squeeze a stream of frosting "hair" falling from the imaginary part down the side of the cake. Continue adding streams of frosting until your cake has a full head of hair, leaving its front, or face, uniced.

6 Using a dab of frosting, glue two cherries on the cake's face for eyes and one for a nose. Then, using clean scissors, carefully cut a piece of fruit roll into the shape of a tongue. Fold tongue in half lengthwise to form a realistic crease down the middle, then unfold and attach under the nose with a dab of icing. (See illustration.)

7 Sprinkle coconut (dandruff flakes) generously down the center part of the head and lightly sprinkle flakes all over the rest of the cake.

Serves: approximately 12 flaky friends

sicko serving suggestion
Stick a sterilized comb or Afro pick in the side of your cake's head!

pathology pound cake

Perfect for snacking on and *for playing coroner, each slice of this lovely loaf looks like a giant tissue sample!*

ingredients

- 1 (16-ounce) box of pound cake mix (plus those ingredients listed on package)
- Vegetable shortening
- Flour
- 1¼ cups seedless strawberry jam
- ½ pint whipping cream
- 3 tablespoons sugar
- 1 (12-ounce) package frozen blueberries, partially thawed

tools you'll need

- Standard loaf pan
- Mixing bowl
- Spoon
- Wire cooling rack
- Electric mixer
- Heavy duty plastic food storage bag
- 2 small serving bowls
- Platter

1 With an adult's help, preheat the oven according to the directions on the package of the pound cake mix.

2 Grease and flour a loaf pan. Mix the cake batter according to the directions on package.

3 Pour a half-inch layer of cake batter into the pan. Then, using a spoon, glop several lines and small pools of jam (blood) over the batter. Pour another half-inch layer of batter on top of the

jam, and again
glop blood on
top. Repeat this
procedure until you
put one final layer of
batter on top, covering
all signs of jam. (You
should have at least
one-quarter cup of
blood left.)

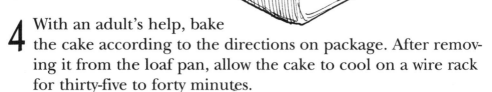

4 With an adult's help, bake
the cake according to the directions on package. After removing it from the loaf pan, allow the cake to cool on a wire rack for thirty-five to forty minutes.

5 With an adult's help, beat the whipping cream until it forms stiff peaks. Add the sugar, then whip it for one minute longer. Using a spoon, gently swirl two tablespoons of the extra blood into the whipped cream, and refrigerate it until you're ready to serve the cake.

6 Place the partially thawed blueberries in a plastic food storage bag. Shut the bag tightly, and with your fist, lightly pound the berries until they are squished, but not completely mush. Pour berries into a bowl, add two tablespoons of jam, and mix well.

7 Slice and arrange the cake on a platter. Place the bloody whipped cream and blueberry blood clots beside the platter for guests to use as toppings.

Serves: 8 to 10 psycho scientists

sicko serving suggestion

Garnish your serving platter with a garland, or little flowers, made of blood-splattered sterile gauze bandage!

BURP!